Another book on angels! What else is there to say about them? I will attempt a few answers. First of all, this will be a quick read. You don't need 200 pages to explore the world of angels. Second, this book provides a basic summary, rooted in a solid biblical and Church tradition. Third, a series of reflection questions are included at the end of each section to help you not only discover angels, but enter into a relationship with your own angel. For a short book, that's a good start.

So, welcome to the world of angels, and may you never leave it!

A lot of people don't believe in angels. How can you believe in something you've never seen? say scientific minds. Aren't angels just a figure of speech that the authors of the Bible used to show God at work? some scripture scholars wonder. Doesn't this subject smack of primitive people seeking a little security through invisible protectors? ask anthropologists.

No one can prove the existence of angels the way we can prove the existence of an invisible particle by measuring its effects. But the existence of angels can be supported by four types of arguments, which I will outline briefly here.

1. The philosophical argument

Many ancient and modern philosophers find it logical to affirm the existence of angels for the following reason. Think about Creation: it appears as a pyramid, going from the more primitive to the complex, from the unconscious to the conscious. At the bottom we find raw materials (stone, water, air); above these are primitive single-cell organisms. Then come the vertebrates, reptiles, birds and mammals. At the apex is the human being, who is made of both matter and spirit. Doesn't this upward movement of beings imply a final level of Creation – pure spirits that are entirely free of matter?

2. Official teaching

This argument works for people who see the Bible as a revelation from God, with the Church as its official interpreter. As we know, angels are found throughout the Bible. Also, the Church includes the angels in its prayer: even at the heart of the Eucharist, the Church invites us to praise God: "with the Angels and all the Saints we declare your glory" (Eucharistic Prayer II).

Of the official Church documents that speak of the existence of angels, we recall the one from the Fourth Lateran Council (1215), which was reclaimed by the First Vatican Council (1870):

> It is an article of faith, firmly established in Scripture and Tradition, and clearly expressed in Christian Doctrine from the beginning, that this spirit world, our Angels, began with time and was created by God. This traditional belief of both the Old and the New Testament was given a more formal and solemn expression in the fourth Lateran Council in 1215: [God] "by his almighty power created together in the beginning of time both creatures, the spiritual and the corporeal, namely the Angelic and the earthly,

and afterwards the human, as it were an intermediate creature, composed of body and spirit."

The *Catechism of the Catholic Church* adds, "The Church venerates the angels who help her on her earthly pilgrimage and protect every human being." (#352)

3. The experience of saints and other witnesses

Many people, including saints down through the ages, have claimed to have seen or heard one or more angels, or at least felt their presence. Here are a few testimonies from the many that are available.

Angela of Foligno
(died in 1309; beatified in 1701)

Angela was a rich noblewoman of Umbria who had a mystical marriage with Christ. She describes a vision she had of Christ surrounded by angels:

> I admired the magnificence surrounding the Lord. Their multitude was resplendent. I saw no end to that multitude in either breadth or length; I saw crowds greater than all our figures. (*An Inquiry into the Existence of Guardian Angels*, p. 254)

Teresa of Avila
(died in 1582; canonized in 1622)

The great Carmelite reformer was completely converted when she heard God say to her, "From now on I don't want you to speak to people, but only to the angels." She had a unique spiritual experience that we see represented in a sculpture by Bernini, which he completed in 1652. Here is how she described her experience in her autobiography:

I saw an angel close by me, on my left side, in bodily form. This I am not accustomed to see, unless very rarely … He was not large, but small of stature, and most beautiful – his face burning, as if he were one of the highest angels, who seem to be all of fire: they must be those whom we call cherubim. Their names they never tell me; but I see very well that there is in heaven so great a difference between one angel and another … that I cannot explain it.

I saw in his hand a long spear of gold, and at the iron's point there seemed to be a little fire. He appeared to me to be thrusting it at times into my heart, and to pierce my very entrails … The pain was so great, that it made me moan; and yet so surpassing was the sweetness of this excessive pain, that I could not wish to be rid of it. The soul is satisfied now with nothing less than God.

The amazing thing is that when St. Teresa died, they removed her heart to expose it in the Carmelite church in Alba de Tormes. The surgeon noticed a transverse tear and burn marks …

Gemma Galgani

(died in 1903; canonized in 1940)

This beautiful woman suffered many trials from a young age. She developed a great friendship with her angel, which helped her along her path to God. She writes,

> The Angel was looking at me so affectionately! And when he was about to go away, and came closer to kiss me on the forehead, I begged him not to leave me again. But he said to me: "I must go." (*An Inquiry into the Existence of Guardian Angels*, p. 304)

Lucia Santos
(died in 2005; started the beatification process in 2008)

Everyone knows the story of the three children of Fatima. In 1916, on a lovely spring day, Lucia was playing with her cousins Jacinta (age 6) and Francisco (age 8). A sudden breeze made them look up. They saw "a very handsome young man about 14 or 15 years old, whiter than snow, whom the sun made transparent, as if he were made of crystal."

This mysterious person drew near to the children and said to them, "Do not be afraid! I am the angel of peace. Pray with me." He came to them two more times, in the summer and in the fall. Each time he urged the children to pray and to make sacrifices "in reparation for the offences, sacrilege and indifference" towards Christ present in the Eucharist. Now there was something new: he introduced himself as the "Angel of Portugal." None of the children spoke of these visits until after the apparitions of the Virgin Mary in 1917.

Gitta Mallasz
(died in 1992)

At the height of the Second World War, four friends living in Budapest decided to get together to discuss existential questions. Three of them – Hanna, Lili and Joseph – were Jewish; the other, Gitta, was Catholic. None of them were especially observant when it came to their faith. During their meeting on November 24, 1943, Hanna suddenly said, "Listen. It is no longer I who is speaking." From that day until November 24, 1944, the four friends were communicating with an angel, and always at the same time: Friday at 3:00 p.m. They later discovered that this was the day and time of Christ's death.

Only Gitta survived the war. Her three friends were taken away to Ravensbrück concentration camp, where they died.

Thirty-three years later, in 1976, Gitta Mallasz transcribed these "revelations" and had them published under the title *Talking with Angels*. In the Preface, the English editor says, "Gitta frequently asserted that she was not the author of this text, but 'merely' the scribe." Despite the book's great success, Gitta never acted like a star or a guru. She lived very simply. Beginning in 1985, she agreed to meet with groups of people who were interested in understanding and living the angel's teachings.

Talking with Angels is fascinating reading, but not easy going. The "mystical" language can be distracting at first. But readers discover as they go along that through this long dialogue with the four young people, the angel offers a path from the self to the other, from Creation to Creator, from fear to the gift of self. In a book containing Gitta's explanations on *Talking with Angels*, she write of the angel:

How does this spiritual being act in me? If he helps me to become more aware of myself and my earthly task; to discover my independence, even from him; to see myself not only as a creature, but as a creator; to set me free from my attachment to the past, but also from my fear of the future; and to live the present moment intensely; to be responsible for myself as well as for the whole universe; then he is a power of divine Love, my equal made of light and I his heavier equal on earth. (*Les dialogues ou le saut dans l'inconnu*, pp. 15–16)

4. Scientific arguments

Scientists tend to refer to angels with a wry smile or with a kind of uneasiness. Indeed, their science is based on what can be measured and quantified – their instruments cannot perceive the existence of the angel, as it is a spirit. And yet, some researchers came into contact with angels by accident, while doing other research.

A significant number of scientists, including Kenneth Ring, professor of psychology at the University of Connecticut, and Melvin Morse, a pediatrician, have done research on near-death experiences, which led them to confirm the existence of spiritual beings. I would like to especially mention the renowned psychiatrist Elisabeth Kübler-Ross. During a visit to a concentration camp, she discovered the "black butterflies" drawn by Jewish children who had been handed a death sentence. Because of this experience she decided to devote her life to accompanying the dying. And that is what she did, thousands of times.

She started her research at the University of Chicago's Pritzker School of Medicine. Her work was highly criticized by the medical staff. In their view, death was a kind of failure and was medicine's enemy number one; being with the dying meant admitting that medicine had its limits. In spite of this opposition, she persevered. In the last few years of her life, she created a centre for children with HIV/AIDS.

Here is an excerpt from an interview she gave to journalist Pierre Jovanovic:

What do you make of angels in these experiences?

— It's normal, because every human being has a guardian angel. An angel is a companion …

Are you in touch with your angels?

— Yes. They help me, guide me, teach me, heal me when I'm sick … You could never survive in this world without your guardian angel.

Do you write down what they say to you?

— No, it's in my heart, and that is enough. You know, I just talk to them, as we are speaking now. I talk to them for hours and hours.

What have they taught you about suffering?

— Suffering is like the Grand Canyon. If you say, "It is so beautiful, we must protect it from wind and storms," it could never be formed by the wind and you would never have the chance to appreciate its beauty.

On the trail of the angels

Step 1

– What is prompting you to read about angels?

– Do you know some people around you who believe in angels? Why do they believe?

– Do you know people who don't believe in angels? Why don't they believe?

– Reflect on your life. Are there events or encounters that cannot be explained, that you chalked up to chance, but that could be due to an angel? Make a note of these.

– Are there times when you have eluded death? What did you learn from this?

– Do you know people who have seen death up close? What do they say about it?

Angels in the Bible

The texts of the Hebrew Scriptures, which became the Christian Old Testament, are foundational for Jews and Christians. They are written using different literary genres: myths, epics, chronicles, narratives, prayers, and more. Angels are present throughout the Old Testament, and in the New Testament as well – from Genesis (the first book), to the Gospels, to Revelation (the last book). What role do angels play? How are they depicted?

Before answering these questions, I must point out that for the authors of the sacred texts – as was the case in the Egyptian, Canaanite and Babylonian cultures – the material world and the spiritual world were intertwined: they had one origin and one destiny. So at all times, the invisible universe could manifest itself in the human universe.

Let's start by looking at some of the terms that are used to describe angels.

Various terms for angels in the Bible

Here are the names used most often to describe these celestial creatures.

Son of God (*benè helohim*)

This name is not related to gender, but is used for those who live in God's world. In a way, they form God's court, just as an earthly ruler is surrounded by his or her highest servants or advisors (see Job 1:6 and Psalms 29 and 89).

Armies, troops (*sabaot*)

This word is found often in the Old Testament – 279 times, in fact – and usually accompanies God's name (the Lord sabaot). For the prophets, this word usually indicates the celestial armies that obey God's orders. When Jesus is arrested, he refers to them, saying, "Do you think that I cannot appeal to my Father, and he will at once send me more than twelve legions of angels?" (Matthew 26:53).

Angels

This is by far the most frequently used term – it appears nearly 400 times. It is the translation of the Greek word *aggelos*, which in turn is a translation of the Hebrew word *malak*, which means "sent" or "messenger." An angel is thus sent by God to carry a message or aid to human beings. The expression "the angel of the Lord" is harder to understand. In a number of biblical passages, it seems to be interchangeable with God: at times the biblical writer says it is the angel of the Lord who is speaking, then says that it is God who is present. (See Genesis 16:10-13; 22:10-18; Exodus 3:2.)

Seraphs (*seraphim*)

This word literally means "the burning ones." The Bible tells us that the Hebrews, during their journey through the desert, were criticizing God. So God sent "poisonous serpents" (*nakash saraph*) to purify his people (Numbers 21:6-8). Later, some seraphs appeared to the prophet Isaiah. These beings, which each had three pairs of wings, guarded in some way the holiness of God in the Temple, and praised God. One of the seraphs took a live coal and touched the prophet Isaiah's mouth to purify him and make him worthy of his mission to carry the word of God (Isaiah 6:1-8).

Cherubim (*keroubim*)

Throughout the Middle East, we find fantastic beings called cherubim at the entrances of temples or near royal thrones. In the temple in Jerusalem, two huge cherubim surrounded "the glory of God," God's mysterious presence in the holiest place within the temple. The prophet Ezekiel, who often spoke of angels, is always at a loss for words to describe them: their "appearance" resembled that of humans or other living beings (1:5, 10, 13) or they "looked like torches moving to and fro … and lightning issued from the fire" (1:13).

Clearly, these are mysterious beings who are near to the glory of the Lord (Ezekiel 10:18). Through them God can be present in all places (Ezekiel 10:22).

Authority, power, strength, sovereignty, throne

These are the names that Paul gives to various celestial creatures, to which some Christians assigned the supervision of the world. Paul names them primarily to say that they are all subject to Christ, in whom all things were created (Colossians 1:16; Ephesians 1:21).

Proper names

Very few angels are called by their proper name in the Bible, as the authors focus more on what the angels do than on their nature or identity, which at times eludes us. Still, three angels are given a name in the book of saints. **Raphael** (the Healing of God) appears only in the Book of Tobit. **Gabriel** (the Power of God) helps the prophet Daniel to understand the meaning of the visions he receives (Daniel 8:16; 9:21) and announces the births of John the Baptist and Jesus (Luke 1:19, 26).

Michael (Who is like God?) is the great fighter against evil forces (Daniel 10:13, 21; 12:1; Jude 9).

The Orthodox Church venerates the seven major archangels: in addition to Raphael, Gabriel and Michael, these are **Uriel** (the Light of God), **Selaphiel** (the Prayer of God), **Jehudiel** (the Glory of God) and **Barachiel** (the Blessings of God). ("El," found at the end of each name, is Hebrew for "God.")

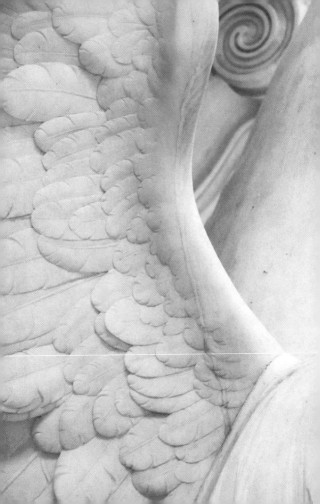

Roles of the angels in the Bible

Announcing

Angels are sent by God to announce extraordinary events. Often, these are unexpected births: the birth of Isaac (Genesis 18:10), Ishmael (Genesis 16:11), Samson (Judges 13:3), John the Baptist (Luke 1:13) and Jesus (Luke 1:31).

Calling

The angel of the Lord calls the young Gideon to free his people (Judges 6:11-23). Gabriel calls Mary to become the mother of the Messiah (Luke 1:26-38).

Adoring

Isaiah sees the seraphim in the temple adoring God while saying, "Holy, holy, holy" (Isaiah 6:3). The writer of the book of Revelation sees "myriads of myriads and thousands of thousands" of angels proclaiming the glory of God and of Christ (Revelation 5:11-12). "Praise the Lord from the heavens; praise him in the heights! Praise him, all his angels; praise him, all his host!" (Psalm 148:1-2).

Accompanying, guarding and protecting

An angel accompanies the servant of Abraham who is seeking a wife for Isaac (Genesis 24:40). God promises Moses that an angel will accompany him during his long journey through the desert (Exodus 32:34). The most striking example is that of Raphael, the angel that accompanies the young Tobias into a foreign land to find a wife (the book of Tobit).

All those who are just are promised the protection of angels:

> Because you have made the Lord
>   your refuge,
> the Most High your dwelling place,
> no evil shall befall you,
> no scourge come near your tent.
>
> For he will command his angels
>   concerning you
> to guard you in all your ways.
> On their hands they will bear you up,
> so that you will not dash your foot
>   against a stone.

Psalm 91:9-12

Delivering

After being attacked by the massive Assyrian army, the city of Jerusalem is saved by an angel who destroys the army (2 Kings 19:35). When the apostle Peter is in prison, an angel comes and delivers him (Acts of the Apostles 12:7-9).

Enlightening

Facing some difficult choices, Joseph receives enlightenment from an angel. The angel tells him not to send away his fiancée, Mary. Later, the angel tells Joseph to flee with Mary and Jesus to Egypt to save the child, and then tells them when it is safe to return home (Matthew 1:19-24; 2:13-22).

Comforting

As he ran from his brother Esau's anger, Jacob saw a multitude of angels climbing and descending between heaven and earth. He understood that God was accompanying him in his escape, which gave him the courage to continue his journey (Genesis 29:1-14).

The great prophet Eli had to flee Queen Jezebel, who wanted to kill him. He lost heart, lay down and asked to die. An angel came and comforted him, bringing him food and letting him rest. Then the angel encouraged him to keep going towards Horeb (1 Kings 19:4-8). And during his agony in the garden, Jesus was comforted by an angel (Luke 22:43).

Revealing

An angel revealed to the prophets Zechariah (1:9, 4:4) and Daniel (8:15-18; 10:21) the meaning of the visions they had received. Angels announced to the shepherds the birth of the Messiah (Luke 2:8-14). To the women who came to the tomb of Jesus to anoint his body, the angels revealed the great mystery of Easter (Matthew 28:2-6; Luke 24:1-8).

In relation to God, the role of the angels is thus to contemplate God, adore God and be in God's service in the fulfillment of history.

The role of the angels in relation to us is to lead us to do what God expects of us: to accomplish our earthly mission by revealing that mission to us, accompanying us on the journey, and helping us along the way.

The Bible leaves a number of questions unanswered: How many angels are there? When were they created? When and why did the fall of angels happen? Some ancient books (the Book of Enoch, the Second Book of Esdras) and certain authors who were inspired by Neoplatonism (Pseudo-Dionysius the Aeropagite) have tried to answer these questions. Kabbalah (Jewish mysticism) and New Age writers have also explored these topics.

On the trail of the angels

Step 2

– Read the Book of Tobit in the Bible.

– What struck you as you read the text?

– What does this text teach you about angels in general?

– Which qualities of the angel Raphael speak to you the most?

My guardian angel

Of course we can pray to the Virgin Mary or Saint Francis or Padre Pio. But anyone can pray to them! That means they have a lot to do. Could there be a spiritual being for each one of us, a kind of spiritual alter ego? That's what certain biblical passages, as well as a long-standing religious tradition, tell us.

In the Bible we read about angels who seem to watch over certain people. An angel delivers the apostle Peter when he is in prison (Acts of the Apostles 12:7-15). An angel who knows the centurion Cornelius, a pagan, says to him, "Cornelius, your prayer has been heard and your alms have been remembered before God" (Acts 10:31). The same angel sets up a meeting between Cornelius and Peter (Acts 10:32-33).

The classic reference to guardian angels is found in the words of Jesus: "Take care that you do not despise one of these little ones; for, I tell you, in heaven their angels continually see the face of my Father in heaven" (Matthew 18:10).

My guardian angel walks with me along my journey, from my birth until my passage through death and into the full presence of God. (For a remarkable image depicting this passage, see Hieronymous Bosch's painting entitled *Ascension to the Light*, painted in the year 1500.) My guardian angel has only one desire: to guide me towards my total fulfillment. To achieve that goal, my angel is ready to offer me the services described earlier in our discussion of the role of angels in the Bible: to protect me, enlighten me, comfort me, and so on.

Since each person has his or her own guardian angel, I can pray to another person's angel as well. For example, if I know I will be having a difficult conversation with someone, I can pray to their guardian angel, asking the angel to prepare the other person for the conversation by inspiring them to bring a listening and peaceful presence to our time together.

In his poem "Guardian Angel," Cardinal Newman writes,

> My oldest friend, mine from the hour
>   When first I drew my breath;
> My faithful friend, that shall be mine,
>   Unfailing, till my death;
> Thou hast been ever at my side;
>   My Maker to thy trust
> Consign'd my soul, what time He framed
>   The infant child of dust.
> … O Brother of my soul,
>   When my release shall come;
> Thy gentle arms shall lift me then,
>   Thy wings shall waft me home.

On the trail of the angels

Step 3

– Read the following passages from the Gospel of Luke:

- the birth of Jesus (Luke 2:1-21)
- the announcing of the resurrection (Luke 24:1-12)

– What is the role of angels in these two stories?

– In these passages, who believes in angels and who refuses to believe?

– How does this reflection shed light on the role of angels in your own life?

Unusual questions about angels

1. Do angels have a gender?

A passage in Genesis tells us that "the sons of God saw that they were fair; and they took wives for themselves of all that they chose" (Genesis 6:2). Were these sons of God angels? Be careful! The texts in Genesis are myths – they seek to answer basic human questions (Where did we come from? Why does evil exist? and so on). They do not answer these questions by using philosophical arguments, but by telling a story. The context here is the degradation of God's creation, which God will rectify by sending the Flood (Genesis 6:5-8).

In the Gospel, Jesus says, "For in the resurrection they neither marry nor are given in marriage, but are like angels in heaven" (Matthew 22:30). This is not a question of looking down on sexuality. Jesus is simply saying that our spiritual selves will meet as the angels do, on another plane, where gender is no longer relevant.

2. Do angels eat?

The well-loved hymn "Panis Angelicus" (Latin for "the bread of angels") is one we still hear at Mass from time to time. (You can find some excellent recordings of it on YouTube.) The title is taken from a hymn by St. Thomas Aquinas (1225–1274) on the Eucharist. The full phrase is "the bread of angels has become the bread of mankind." If angels do not have bodies, they should not need food. But a universal law seems to be at work here: all living creatures must eat.

If angels must eat, then what kind of food do they eat? It is not going too far to say that angels are nourished by ... presence! We, too, need not only bread but also the loving presence of others so we can live. The angels feed on the most intense presence of all – God's presence. From God they receive everything: being and the joy of being. They are truly nourished by the God they contemplate.

3. Do angels have wings?

Apart from the cherubim and seraphs mentioned in the visions of the prophets, the angels in the Bible do not usually have wings. They often appear as people "in dazzling clothes" (Luke 24:4; Acts 10:30). As we read earlier, Teresa of Avila saw one who was "not large, but small of stature, and most beautiful." To Catherine Labouré (d. 1876), the angel appeared as "a child dressed in white, around 4 or 5 years old."

Georgette Faniel (d. 2002), a Montreal mystic and stigmatic, describes her guardian angel this way:

> He was wearing a white tunic. But you can't compare his beauty to human beauty. He is beyond all that, in his features, his face, in everything. I've never seen such a handsome man. (*An Inquiry into the Existence of Guardian Angels*, p. 207)

Artists have tended to put wings on angels, probably to highlight their ability to fly and their role as messengers. Thanks to the example of these artists, Fra Angelico could paint on angels' wings exquisite rainbows, which are signs of peace, and the anonymous sculptors of the Middle Ages could form the angels' mysterious smiles.

4. How many angels are there?

Nobody really knows. Some say that a third of the angels fell with Lucifer and that humans would be called to replace them in heaven. That means there are more angels than humans. According to the vision of the book of Revelation, there are so many angels, they cannot be counted (5:11). In Pseudo-Dionysius the Areopagite's classification in *The Celestial Hierarchy*, the angels would be divided into nine choirs:

1st hierarchy: seraphs, cherubim, thrones

2nd hierarchy: dominions, powers, authorities

3rd hierarchy: principalities, archangels, angels

5. Do countries have their own angel?

In speaking to the prophet Daniel, an angel mentioned the "prince of the kingdom of Persia" and of "Michael, your prince" (Daniel 10:13, 21). The angel who appeared to the children of Fatima introduced himself as "the angel of Portugal." In apocalyptic literature (which contains revelations on the end times), each nation has an angel that watches over it.

On the trail of the angels

Step 4

– Do you ever pray to your guardian angel?

– If you would like to do so, you may use the traditional prayers found in the following pages, or create your own.

A child's prayer

Angel of God, my guardian dear,
to whom God's love commits me here,
ever this day be at my side
to light and guard, to rule and guide.
Amen.

A morning prayer

My good Angel, you come from heaven;
God has sent you to take care of me.
O shelter me under your wings.
Lighten my path, direct my steps.
Do not leave me, stay quite near me
and defend me against the spirit of evil.
But above all come to my help
in the last struggle of my life.
Deliver my soul so that with you
it may praise, love and contemplate
the goodness of God forever and ever.
Amen.

An evening prayer

Dear Angel,

in His goodness God gave you to me

to guide, protect, and enlighten me,

and to bring me back to the right way when I go astray.

Encourage me when I am disheartened,

and instruct me when I err in judgment.

Help me to become more Christ-like,

and so some day to be accepted

into the company of Angels and Saints in heaven.

Amen.

A couple's prayer

Angel of God who watches over us,

God in his great goodness has entrusted us to you.

Enlighten us, guide us,

govern us, protect us,

and make us one in this world and the next.

Amen.

A prayer for friends

Guardian Angel,

watch over those whose names
 you can read in my heart.

Guard over them with every care

and make their way easy
 and their labours fruitful.

Dry their tears if they weep;

sanctify their joys;

raise their courage if they weaken;

restore their hope if they lose heart,

their health if they be ill,

truth if they err,

repentance if they fail.

Amen.

Prayer on the feast of the Holy Guardian Angels (October 2)

O God, who in your unfathomable providence

are pleased to send your holy Angels to guard us,

hear our supplication as we cry to you,

that we may always be defended by their protection

and rejoice eternally in their company.

Through our Lord Jesus Christ, your Son,

who lives and reigns with you in the unity of the Holy Spirit,

one God, for ever and ever.

Amen.

By way of conclusion

In this age of the Internet, Facebook and Twitter, aren't angels obsolete? I give the last word to theologian Yves Cattin:

> In my electronic messages, it is no longer a question of saying something, but of writing for the sake of writing, writing to exist. Thus pure communication was born, communication for the sake of communication, without needing something to say. We have invented the perfect angel, the definitive angel …

Also, in this new era, the angels are calling us to a new Annunciation. They are urging us to renounce the gods of politics and entertainment, of money and economics, of technology and science, of power and glory. They say that God and the human person are not found there, in the misleading promise of a life without death … In this way, the paths of the angels open to us once more, in the driving passion of a new world. *(Les anges et leur image au Moyen Âge,* pp. 282–290)

Sources
"Angels." *Anchor Bible Dictionary*, 1992.

The Holy Bible (New Revised Standard Version). Toronto: Collins Publishers, 1989.

The Life of St. Teresa of Jesus, of the Order of Our Lady of Carmel. Written by Herself. David Lewis, trans. Third edition enlarged. New York: Benziger Bros, 1904.

Revised Roman Missal. Ottawa: Canadian Conference of Catholic Bishops, 2011.

Yves Cattin and Philippe Faure. *Les anges et leur image au Moyen Âge*. Paris: Zodiaque, 1999.

Jean Daniélou. *Les anges et leur mission*. Ciney: Éditions de Chevetogne, 1951.

Gitta Mallasz. *Talking with Angels*. Einsiedeln, Switzerland: Daimon, 1988.

Pierre Jovanovic. *An Inquiry into the Existence of Guardian Angels: A Journalist's Investigative Report*. New York: M. Evans and Company, 1995.

Giorgi Rosa. *Angels and Demons in Art*. Los Angeles: Getty Publications, 2003.

http://www.catholic.org

http://www.catholictradition.org/Angels/angels2.htm

http://www.newmanreader.org/works/verses/verse167.html

© 2012 Novalis Publishing Inc.

Cover: Quatre-Quarts
Cover photo: © iStockphoto
Layout: Danielle Dugal and Amy Eaton
Interior photos: 2, 22, 48-49: iStockphoto ; 28, 30-31, 32, 34, 37, 45, 50, 62-63, 65, 66, 68-69, 70, 78, 80-81, 82, 91, 94: Crestock; 96: Wikimedia Commons
Translation: Anne Louise Mahoney

Originally published in French by Les Éditions Novalis in 2011.

Published by Novalis

Publishing Office	Head Office
10 Lower Spadina Avenue, Suite 400	4475 Frontenac Street
Toronto, Ontario, Canada	Montréal, Québec, Canada
M5V 2Z2	H2H 2S2

www.novalis.ca

Library and Archives Canada Cataloguing in Publication

> Madore, Georges
> Angels / Georges Madore ; Anne Louise
> Mahoney, translator.
>
> (Faith moments)
> Translation of: Les anges.
> ISBN 978-2-89646-467-8
>
> 1. Angels. I. Mahoney, Anne Louise
> II. Title. III. Series: Faith moments
>
> BL477.M3213 2012   202'.15   C2012-901600-4

Printed in Canada.

All rights reserved. No part of this publication may be reproduced, stored in a retrieval system, or transmitted in any form, or by any means, electronic, mechanical, photocopying, recording, or otherwise, without the written permission of the publisher.

We acknowledge the financial support of the Government of Canada through the Canada Book Fund for business development activities.

5 4 3 2 1   16 15 14 13 12